V8

A National Motor Museum
Trust book by
Michael Frostick

Beaulieu Books

First published in 1979

ISBN 0901564 400

Published by
DALTON WATSON LTD.
76 Wardour Street, London W1V 4AN
in association with
THE NATIONAL MOTOR MUSEUM TRUST

Photosetting and Litho Platemaking by Star Illustration Works Ltd.

Printed in England by The Lavenham Press Ltd.

Introduction

This is not a technical book about the V8 engine, as the quickest and most cursory glance will show. It is rather a nostalgic survey of those cars which have employed engines of that configuration, with, hopefully, enough information for us to see in retrospect where they fit into the scheme of things in the motoring world.

The engine is the heart of a car, and like the human heart provides not only the power but a good deal of the character as well. In human beings, we link with the heart ideas on warmth of character, qualities of love and hate, and much else besides, and we may usefully make an analogy in the case of the car. A large powerful man of good heart may be thought better company than a frail character of little power and even less magnetism. Both probably have their own virtues; and in the world of cars, this book, which sets out to extol the virtues of the V8, is not unmindful of those lesser vehicles which have also played their part – and without which most of us would not have become motorists in the first place.

The V8s are the nobility of cars; and the fact that during the last war they joined with all classes in the effort to win, and that in the years since there has been a certain levelling, a certain diminution of splendour, then it only goes to show how closely our cars are linked to ourselves.

Not every V8 is here, considerations of space, and its companion cost, have ruled that out; but the selection is representative, and within these covers are displayed the V8s in all their glory.

Contents

Acknowledgment

I should like to give particular thanks to the several people who have been particularly helpful in the compilation of this book. Firstly my friends Griffith Borgeson and Michael Sedgwick, both of whom have a wider knowledge of American Cars than I do and who helped considerably on a number of obscure points. There is then Steve Clark, who runs the Ford photographic unit, and without whose help the pages on the famous Ford V8 of the thirties would look blank indeed; and lastly the library staff at Beaulieu who, although they have an obvious vested interest, went out of their way to help me dig and delve for unlikely pictures and even more unlikely snippets of information.

Photographs are from the Photographic Library of The National Motor Museum with the exception of the following:

Ford Motor Company Limited. Pages: 30 top, 32, 33 top, 36, 46, 47, 48, 49, 50 top and bottom, 51, 52, 96, 97, 99.

G. N. Georgano. Pages: 24 top, 38 top, 56 bottom, 59 top, 68 top, 80 centre, 81 top.

I.P.C. Business Press Ltd. 1978. Page 33 centre and bottom.

Hans Otto Neubauer collection. Page 18 top.

Strother McMinn collection. Page 23.

Michael Ware. Pages: 102, 103.

Donald J. Summar collection. Page 13 bottom.

John Player and Company Limited. Page 110.

Stan Yost. Page 18 bottom.

CHAPTER ONE

Early Days

At the very beginning of motoring, when cars were made with great skill but by simple methods, the design of the engine, provided it was sound, presented no great problems. In very general terms it was as easy (or difficult) to make a V8 as it was to make almost anything else – and there was practically nothing that someone wasn't trying somewhere. The internal combustion engine, and indeed the motor car when all is said and done, is not an invention; and nobody knows for sure who didn't invent it. It was a development of a great many, then current, ideas. Trains had arrived, and steam carriages had run on the roads, the gas engine was well established, and quite a number of men were clever enough to want to put two and two together and make a motor car.

The need which was felt, and which has subsequently transformed civilisation, was for mobile power, for self-propelled vehicles, as governments and lawyers like to have it. If a gas engine could be made to run on liquid fuel, which could be carried on the vehicle, then the problem was solved. Steam and electricity, of course, could provide the same, or similar, answers; but it was the engine that ran on petrol gas, that won the day. Daimler and Benz, who only lived a few miles apart but didn't know each other, are usually thought of as "the inventors" of the motor car. They were indeed the men who saw that it was not a question of making one, but of making many. But there were others before them, Lenoir in France, and Markus in Austria, for example.

However it is sensible to take the beginning of the motor car as 1885 when both Benz and Daimler had vehicles in their workshops if not actually on the road. Single cylinder affairs of very little power they set the pattern. Others followed, and by 1892 when the Duryea brothers built the first American car everyone was at it. Then came the race for power; and in many ways it really was a race, for it was racing that made the need for power so urgent. As soon as anyone managed to get a car he was all for racing his next door neighbour to the end of the street, and then to the end of the town. Not long after, it was from town to town; and it was in the famous, but ill-fated, race that should have gone from Paris to Madrid; but ended, after the most frightful carnage, at Bordeaux that the first V8 appeared.

This was the work of a Frenchman, Clément Ader who was, among other things, a telephone engineer, and a maker of steam engines for aeroplanes! His company rejoiced in the name of Societé Industrielle des Téléphones-Voitures Automobiles système Ader, and was founded just outside Paris in 1900. It was 1903 when the Paris-Madrid took place, and Mr. Ader must have been among the first manufacturers to believe in the value of racing, for his firm entered no less than seven cars, a V-twin, three V4's and three V8's (whose engines were in fact a pair of the V4's put together). All of them reached Bordeaux where the race was stopped by government order; but the widespread interest in it must have brought the V8 configuration to the notice of most enthusiasts and many of the public as well. Some historians feel that the next giant in this field, the V8 Darracq, is more important. This was the car which not only claimed the World's Speed Record in 1905, after a timed run along the main road between Arles and Salon in the south of France; but later went to America, where, driven by Louis Chevrolet among others, it gave an even more startling performance. It must also have brought the V8 idea to the notice of engineers in the United States, for had not Cadillac introduced a production V8 for 1915 interest in such engines might have disappeared for a long time.

No more was heard of the Darracq record breaker after its first bold efforts, and Clement Ader went out of business in 1907. The flag was carried on in Europe by the Count De Dion and his engineer partner

Mr. Bouton; and they made the first production V8 in 1910. There was quite a lot wrong with it, and they modified their designs continuously over the years; but by 1913 they had got it right, and their last V8 cars based on that year's E series, stayed in production until 1923. The Americans on the other hand went at the thing in a much bigger way, and from 1914 to 1929 for example, the only engines Cadillac produced were V8s.

From this we see that the first advantage offered by the V8 was one of power – more power for a given weight. At first it produced rather rough engines, as everyone was using a four cylinder crankshaft (180°) which gives a nasty vibration when used with a V8 called, in engineering terms, a rotating couple. A man called Heldt suggested that instead of the obvious 90° vee which everyone was using, a 60° would offer a considerable advantage – it did; but not nearly enough. It was not until Cadillac introduced the 90° crankshaft in 1923, that the V8 engine began to show that smoothness which was, for the Americans at all events, to be the big reason for using it. This allowed the V8 to become a challenge to the straight eight – one of the most attractive engines ever.

So the point of emphasis changed from Europe to America, from power to smoothness – not to mention a good deal of snob appeal from time to time. Henry Ford came along in 1932 and revolutionised the scene completely; but that is to go too far ahead for the moment. Here we are concerned with the big and successful V8s of the years between the dawn of motoring and the outbreak of the Second World War.

This is the 1916 Daniels with what was the current fashion in coachwork for American sports cars. The engine was a Herschell-Spillman unit and the cars, made in very small numbers, were the brainchild of G. E. Daniels who set up on his own after being president of Oakland.

Seen here in the tragic Paris-Madrid race of 1903 is one of the V8 Ader cars – three were entered. They were the first V8s to be made and the engine was in fact two of the Ader V4s put together. Ader, a telephone engineer, was a great exponent of the 'V' form; and all of the seven cars he entered in the race reached Bordeaux, where it was stopped. This is No. 16 driven by Valentin. It was the search for power that first made the V8 interesting, and nowhere was this search more anxiously carried out than in preparations for this event. Public interest in the motorcar was becoming widespread, and manufacturers were already alert to the fact that victory in this field was first class publicity. Sadly it was the amount of public interest, and the lack of spectator control, which brought about the carnage on the route, and caused the authorities to have the cars halted at Bordeaux. They had to return to Paris by train and were not even allowed to drive to the station – but had to be drawn by horses, so great was the public outrage. A sad end to the first notable V8 outing.

More interesting, more sedate and more unusual was the first Rolls-Royce V8 – the Legalimit. Two versions were made, of which the one illustrated here is the first. Competition from the electric brougham as a town vehicle, and the battle between police and the motorist, decided Royce to make a car which, in the first version, was to provide a town car; and in the second, when the engine came out from under the floorboards and into an ordinary bonnet, was to be capable of 20mph up hill and down dale but no more – hence the name, a contraction of 'legal limit'. The interesting thing about the V8 engine was its "square" dimensions of 83mm for both bore and stroke, and its low gear ratios. There were three forward speeds, but the car would start in top on ordinary level ground. Very few of them were made for despite the publicity and the excitement at the 1905 motor show Royce had his mind on the Silver Ghost; and although the battle with the police has hardly abated to this day, they have at least had to give up accusing motorists of going too fast because they cannot catch a car when they run after it.

The relatively small overall size of the 1905 200hp Darracq give no indication of its enormous engine capacity, totalling 22,518cc. To make it, Alexandre Darracq used two blocks of his 1904 Gordon Bennett racer's engine to form a V-8 unit developing 200hp. All sixteen valves were overhead. The chassis was a very light affair with a wheelbase of only 7ft 10ins and a wide track of 5ft 1in. Victor Hemery set a new Land Speed Record of 109.65 on the Arles-Salon road in December 1905. The first photo shows Algernon Lee Guinness before starting his run at the 1906 Ostend Speed Trials at which he covered a flying kilometre at 117.66mph, while the second is a close-up of the engine.

It was 1906 before the Adams Manufacturing Co. of Bedford came up with a V8. They had previously been making small cars, some of them known as Adams-Hewitts because they had been designed by an American called Hewitt. When it came to the V8 however, they moved into the luxury class, but continued to use the system of pedal operated epicyclic gears that gave them the slogan "Pedals to Push – That's All". Sadly, for all their enterprise, the V8 was very short lived and the company went out of production with the outbreak of war in 1914.

In 1906 the celebrated French firm of Antoinette, who were best known for their aeroplanes and aero engines, showed a 32hp V8 at the Paris Salon; and it is this engine that went into the Adams car. There were some changes as it crossed the channel, for the French version had automatic inlet valves whereas Adams converted them to a mechanical operation : though it would take more than this to explain the curious placing of the sparking plugs.

In 1910 De Dion Bouton produced the first production V8 to be made in Europe, and followed this first design with two others, in as many years. In 1912, which is when this car was made, they produced yet another new V8, with monobloc cylinders in two banks, and thermo-syphon cooling. It was an early example of putting a large engine in a small car and thereby providing a startling amount of power. Many of these early cars were very handsome; but one could hardly apply that description to this model, with its tiny door and its' driver already crowding in on the already overcrowded rear compartment. The coachbuilder is not known, but the car appears to have run in the Tour de France, which may explain the flag by the windscreen.

Much more handsome is this 1914 version of the successful De Dion Bouton V8. This was the 'E series' which stayed in production until 1923, and at the start of its career even had some competition success. It was 4th in the Targa Florio in 1913, and again in the following year. On the technical side it is sad to recall that the famous suspension system for the rear, which we know even today as the De Dion axle, began to be dropped from the range in 1911; and from that point onwards historians are inclined to suggest that the marque lost all its originality. However, V8s did not abound on every street; and had it not been for the Count De Dion in Europe, and, as we shall see, Cadillac in America we might not have had any V8s at all.

Cadillac, which gets its name from a small town not so far from Detroit, itself named after Le Sieur Antoine de la Mothe Cadillac who came that way in 1701 and was later Governor of Louisiana, has long been one of the great names in American motoring. The company became part of the General Motors group in 1909, and they made their first left-hand drive car in 1914 (which was, in the fashion of the day, the 1915 model) – it was also their first V8. It seems they had a good look at what Mr. Bouton had been making with the Count De Dion's money; and then managed to fulfil the all-time American claim of doing it bigger and better. The illustration here is of a 1921 tourer, property of a Mr. Barrett of Johannesburg, South Africa. In translating the De Dion groundwork into American quantity, if not actually mass, production they managed to give the 5½ litre engine much more power than the French had had, and were soon to set the pattern for the whole of the U.S. luxury market, for by about 1920 there were something like 22 different American manufacturers offering a V8.

Before we get carried away with the new splendours of so many V8 cars flooding the market it is well to remember that there were commercial considerations as well. This 1920 truck, for example, is a Rowe – known as the "Three Ton Speed Truck". Its engine, like that of so many commercial vehicles, was a proprietary affair, a V8 made by Herschell Spillman of North Tonawanda, New York, who also for a short time made private cars, but not V8s.

After successfully making commercial vehicles for five years, Sydney Guy brought out a thoroughly modern luxury passenger car in 1919. It had a 4,072cc side-valve V-8 engine specially designed for the car, and not only full-pressure engine lubrication but automatic chassis lubrication which was activated every time the steering was on full right lock. The Guy guarantee included free inspection at any time during the first two years of the car's life. However, it was undeniably expensive at £1,475 for the tourer illustrated and fewer than 150 were made in a five-year lifetime. It was the first production British V-8, and no others were made until Riley's 8/90 of 1936.

Among the makers who followed Cadillac's lead were a number of small manufacturers such a the King Motor Car Co. (also of Detroit) who from 1915 onwards made V8s. Theirs was a small V8, even by current standards, being of under 4 litres capacity. For a short while they did very well with rather ordinary conventional cars as the photograph shows; but the post war depression hit them, and after moving to a smaller works in Buffalo they ceased manufacture. A number of the cars came to England where the agents were the well known coachbuilders Salmons of Newport Pagnell – who used to make "Tickford" bodies; and indeed put some on the King cars they imported.

If you are inclined to think these days that cars are much of a muchness, you will find that in the early 1920s, in America at least, the same applied. This is a 1922 Lincoln, which Henry M. Leland put into production after he had left Cadillac in 1917. It had a 5.8 litre side-valve engine with full pressure lubrication and was capable of over 70mph. It seems that the styling of the bodies did not match the excellence of the works and Henry Ford took the company over just about the time the car in our picture was made.

The innocent might be forgiven for thinking that they had seen this before; but they would be wrong. This is a 1923 Cole. The V8 model was introduced in 1915 and was their best known car. It had a 5.4 litre Northway engine and was expensive, later models had Westinghouse air springs housed in unsightly cylinders by the bumpers. This example gives a good impression of the then current American fashions, the big lamps, here with the addition of parking lights built into the same case, a big well stiffened hood, flat heavy mudwings, and in this case a bumper well before it became common practice. The big bars on the radiator cap were also very usual at the time, being on several General Motors products as well. The photograph is contemporary and it may be noticed that the car carries "trade" plates.

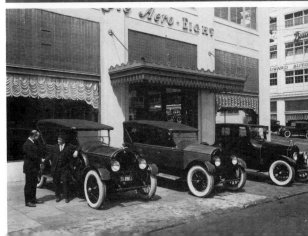

Again 1923 and again Cole. An imposing showroom with a line up of cars outside. The Aero Eight was by British rating of the day a 39.2hp car, but not many of them reached the shores of Great Britain. On the right of the picture is one of the hideous coupés that were in vogue in America at the time; but in terms of sheer horror nothing could match the names that the Cole Motor Car Co. of Indianapolis gave their models – Tourosine and Sportosine being among them.

James Cunningham, Son, and Company, Incorporated, of Rochester in the State of New York, were motor makers of some quality; so it is not surprising that they too, from 1916 onwards, were devotees of the V8 engine. They were as much coachbuilders as car makers, and built their luxury models a few at a time so that there was very little "standard" about any of them – save their mechanics. The engine was a 6 litre V8 said to develop about 100bhp, which was a lot for 1924 or thereabouts, when this picture was taken. The Dual-Cowl Phaeton was a well established American type; but the fancy wings and lights are anything but ordinary.

The Peerless V8 and the mixture as before. The Peerless was one of the great cars of America, being ranked with Packard and Pierce-Arrow as the "Three Ps". The V8 always looked very like Cadillacs even in this year, 1924. When the design had been up-dated the resemblance remained. Really more interesting than the car, in this photograph, is the showroom, with all the contemporary style displayed and not too many cars to get in the way. The cars were expensive and business was good – they sold 5,000 cars in 1923 – so an air of decent luxury must be expected.

Hollywood in 1930, though the surroundings are not so important to us. The car, a Cadillac V8, as is all too clearly proclaimed on its tie-bar. The general "just short of Hispano" shape was current in most American products of that time, and in this case the coachwork is clearly "custom" with the falling line from radiator cap to running board also much in vogue, though the engine-turned finish was far less usual. Fans of the "Great Days of Hollywood" must be left to tell us the names of the stars, and the films they were in; but the plot thickens on close inspection, as the handsome rotter in the back seat is discerned. "Once aboard the lugger . . . ."

Also Hollywood at the turn of the decade, this shot of a current Lincoln (comfortably after Henry Ford had taken over) shows the quality preserved. The car is a town sedan, the people a mystery which is not helped by a single caption on the back of the photograph which says, simply and confusingly, "John Wayne". If you believe that you'll believe anything.

Meanwhile Europe was not idle for in 1931 the N.A.G. company, who were probably best known for their buses and commercials, produced a 4.5-litre 100bhp V8. Considering its date it is a very advanced looking car which might well pass muster as a 1934 model. N.A.G. also put their V8 into a front-wheel-drive chassis; but that never got into production, and in 1934 they gave up making private cars altogether and turned their interests back to commercials.

One of the only two road-going cars which Harry Armenius Miller ever made. World famous for his racing cars, and the engines which powered them, Harry Miller was one of the great eccentrics of life; but at the same time one of the great sages of automobile engineering. This particular car was made to the order of Philip Challenor, a millionaire. It has a 4.9 litre V8 engine (in reality two Miller 'fours' on a common crank-case) with a single overhead camshaft to each block. Unfortunately Harry Miller had one of his not infrequent bankruptcies before it was finished, and the work was completed by a Pasadena coachbuilder, Gerard Kirchoff. Said to be capable of 135mph its engine produced no less than 325bhp, and the car must represent one of the highlights of V8 history.

Miller built two four-wheel-drive cars to the order of Walter A Olen, a director of the Four-Wheel-Drive truck company in about 1932. They used patents from the FWD company and no doubt a good deal of Harry Miller's expertise in respect of the front-wheel-drive part of it.

The cars first ran at Indianapolis in 1932 with their V8 engines, which must have been not dissimilar from that in the preceding sports car. By 1934 both cars had been fitted with four cylinder engines; but they continued to run at Indianapolis up to 1937, after which one of them at least, was used for hill climbs. They were not road cars and the button on the steering wheel is not a horn; but a "kill button" for stopping the engine by shorting out the magneto.

The Derby was hardly a typical French car, and this 1934 V8 with an almost American roadster body was hardly even typical of the firm. One of the great pleasures of the years between the wars was the survival of a number of healthily eccentric small companies, going their own way, and making a reasonable, if not resounding, profit out of their enthusiastic adherents. Derby was just such a company, situated among countless others on the banks of the Seine near Paris. They began in 1921 and for many years made light cars with the usual French proprietary engines. Mrs. Gwenda Stewart helped to make them famous with record breaking activities in a car called the Derby Miller, which was a good deal more Miller than Derby. It was this car that led them to Front-Wheel-Drive and among their last offerings was this 11Cv L8 of 1933 which used a small 2 litre V8 engine.

The Stoewer company from Stettin went out of production on the outbreak of the Second World War; up to then they had been prolific and predictable German car makers. This front-wheel-drive V8, the Greif, dates from 1935, and is in general a typical German car of the period, with its solid body, its twin side-mounts and Front-Wheel-Drive, which was fast gaining ground in the Third Reich as the proper way to do things. A total of 825 Greif V8s were made. Some V8 cars also appeared at the 1934 Brussels show under the name of D.S. for Dewaet-Stoewer, Mr. Dewaet being the importer.

Designed by Hans Ledwinka, a man almost as important as Porsche, the rear engined Tatras made motoring history when they were introduced with this model in 1934. He started off to design a body on truly aerodynamic principles, and the rear engine configuration sprang naturally from this. The use of a V8 reduced overhang, and air cooling reduced weight – there was nothing that was not logical about the car, though trying to go fast round corners might make the average reader question the truth of that statement. Almost more interesting than the car itself is the fact that with various necessary and sensible modifications, it has remained in production up to the present time; and another version will be found later in the book. Along with the cars of Sir Dennistoun Burney (which did not use V8s) these were the first bold efforts to bring aerodynamic principles and the logical use of a rear engine into practical everyday use. Of the two, the Tatra must be regarded as the more sensible – and certainly the most long-lasting. Its faults were perhaps best summed up by two R.A.F. Officers who had a "captured" one for use between their airfields in Denmark at the end of the war. They called it "God", for it moved in mysterious ways its wonders to perform.

If the Ford V8 can have been said to popularise that type of engine, then the Cord increased its snob appeal by an equal amount. Leaving the engine configuration out of it altogether the Cord 810 of 1937 was one of the all time greats. The makers, who also controlled Duesenberg, Auburn and the Lycoming Engine Company, and were themselves controlled by Erret Lobban Cord himself, commissioned the design from Gordon Buehrig. With Front-Wheel-Drive, retractable headlamps, an electrically controlled gearshift, as well as its generally futuristic appearance, the Cord in 1937 was way ahead of its time. It also brought many European overtones to American design generally.

Sadly in an effort to increase sales a supercharged model was then made available. The supercharger would hardly have blown the head off a puff ball; but it sounded good. Unfortunately they decided to put "outside exhausts" in the manner of the 540K Mercedes through the sides of the elegant bonnet, and all but ruined one of the best pieces of industrial design the automotive industry has yet produced. But the shape was there and the fact that ever since the company went broke (which it did just before the Second World War) people have been trying to revive the shape, if not the car itself, says more than any mere commentary can.

If one is going to say that the original Cord conception was not improved by the addition of "outside exhausts" then the imagination boggles at the choice of words to describe this essay in "Things to Come" (which fortunately never really arrived).

Using a Cord V8 engine in a special chassis frame, Rust Heinz, son of millionaire H.J. (Beanz Meanz) Heinz, engaged the services of the Californian coachbuilding firm of Bohman & Schwartz to make this "Phantom Corsair" in 1936. Its bench-type front seat was made to accommodate four abreast, and there were two rear seats described by the knowledgeable as "uninhabitable". The doors opened by electricity, so if the battery went flat with luck you couldn't get in, or without luck you probably couldn't get out.

It was planned to put the thing into production to sell at the then somewhat astronomic price of $14,700. Young Heinz was sadly killed in a road accident (not in this car) and the only example now reposes in the Harrah collection.

All along as we have seen General Motors, particularly under their Cadillac name, have been pioneers of the top quality V8's. In the latter half of the twenties they sought to widen the "Caddy" market by the introduction of a slightly less expensive car to be known as the La Salle (another French pioneer General). Using the same body shells in 1937, when this car was made, as certain Buick and Oldsmobile models, the car nevertheless represented the best of G.M. thinking with its "turret top" and other refinements – and, of course, the famous General Motors V8 engine.

The repercussions of the Ford V8, which has the next part of this book to itself, were widespread. Foundry techniques were developed everywhere – though for certain smaller manufacturers this was not important. It was middle thirties before the British really got the V8 bug, and among the first was Riley. They offered a V8, two of the four cylinder blocks on a common crankcase (the old fashioned method) of which very few were made and even fewer survive. This car is a Riley "special" but powered with one of the V8 engines – seen here at Prescott in 1970 and looking suitably chunky.

Having had the V8 idea, Riley had second thoughts and decided to go for the top of the market. They formed Autovia Cars Ltd., and had a fresh stab at a V8 this time using two 1½ litre blocks to give them a 100 bhp 2.8 litre car. On this they offered a good looking saloon, with the then fashionable twin sidemounts, a preselector gearbox, and an interesting price of just under £1000. They also offered a rather more clumsy looking limousine – of which at least one was made, and with the coming of the Second World War the project folded.

Much nearer the Ford in conception was the Flying Standard of 1937. Sir John Black, then the managing director, evidently seeing what Ford had done decided that there was room in his range too for a side-valve V8 – which could use the same body shells as his 12 hp model and indeed most of the other components. The result was an interesting car very much in the Ford V8 mould, with lots of power and flexibility at low cost. Sadly the war clouds were gathering and there was not time to develop the idea, although a few were sold.

There were a spate of cars in the late thirties using the Ford V8 engine, Jensen and Allard to name but two. It is not surprising therefore that when Raymond Mays, who was having a great success with the ERA racing cars, decided to make a sports car bearing his name he should think of a V8 engine. It is also not surprising that such a patriot should want that engine to be British – and he therefore turned to the Standard. Only 5 were built; but here is Mays himself on Brighton front during the 1939 R.A.C. Rally.

And here is the Standard V8 engine in one of the Raymond Mays cars, from which its general similarity with the Ford can be seen. There was not much room for it hence the cunning removable panel to enable you to get a plug spanner on number one plug. As we come nearly to the end of the pre-war cars it is an interesting side line that accessibility is not the V8's stongest point, and even today, and even with Rolls-Royce, that fact remains.

The Germans did not rush into the V8 market though their best engineers were much concerned with the V configuration in terms of Grand Prix cars and their natural successors aero engines. However Horch (part of the Auto Union combine) did offer a V8, as well as their famous straight eight, and here is a 1939 type 930 with standard saloon coachwork. The interior is a good example of the German style of the period though we must take it that the clock on a wooden panel is a later addition to hide a hole left by the removal of some other instrument. The main gearlever is marked with four speeds and reverse and the smaller lever operates an overdrive with high and low positions.

CHAPTER TWO

Workhorse Extraordinary

As time rolls on, views of history change; and Henry Ford, who was once remembered for putting up a fight against the Selden Patents, or of hurtling across a frozen lake at over ninety miles an hour, or making the model "T" and saying you could have it any colour you liked as long as it was black, can now be better thought of as the man who put the V8 on the map. With it he provided more motive power, for more different purposes, than almost any other single engine; and one could almost say the Second World War would have been lost without it.

Henry himself, of course, in the manner of great men of industry, did little but give orders; but he was surrounded by able men in the early thirties, not the least of whom was Charles Sorensen. It is to him as much as to anyone that we owe the Ford V8; but some of the background is less than clear.

When the famous model "T" had run out of breath commercially, Ford replaced it by a four cylinder car of conventional design, and considerable merit; but the fact remained that his competitors in general, and Chevrolet in particular, were offering six cylinder models of much more refinement at very little extra cost. Ford could very well have joined the six-cylinder brigade, and left it at that; but he believed he could do better. So much is clear and straightforward, what is less clear, is whether Sorensen developed the techniques, which revolutionised the production of V8 engines, because his boss said he had to; or whether, because the techniques proved possible, Ford staked his all on the possibility. At all events, the cost of rebuilding the foundry at Rouge River was over fifty million dollars, so whatever else, no one lacked faith.

There is a widespread idea that the triumph of the Ford V8 stems from the fact that Sorensen found a way to cast a V8 block in one piece; but this is not really true. General Motors had been building monobloc V8s back in 1929, though they did not do so in great numbers; and of course the Lancia Dilambda was also a monobloc, though of exceptionally narrow angle. What Sorensen, with his colleagues, and particularly a man named Hansen, did was to find a way to mass produce monobloc V8s, which meant turning all the previously held foundry ideas upside-down. Whereas General Motors with Oldsmobile had been making a little more than 5000 a year at best, Ford set out to make, and succeeded in making, 3000 a day! They also made a cast V8 crankshaft; and these two put together were what cost Ford his millions.

The outcome was a predictable triumph, a V8 for the masses, competitive in price with the market alternatives, it raced ahead of them in performance. The first V8 Ford, the 18F, which appeared in 1932 with a capacity of 3622cc, was able to move the car, which weighed a modest 23 cwt, at over 80mph; and provide the truly astonishing 0-50 time of 12 seconds. On those figures alone it outshone most sports cars; and with its synchromesh gearbox, and very little need for the ordinary motorist to change gear at all, it swept all before it.

Over the years like Topsy "it just growed" getting more power to cope with more weight. It was made in Ireland, in Dagenham; and there were Ford V8s of various types all over Europe, it became a staple power unit in many specials, and small volume luxury cars; and in the war, powered everything from Bren carriers to boats.

From 1945 onwards it had another brief spell of glory in the Ford Pilot in Great Britain, and a number of handsome continentals, ending up in the Comète, which was the father of the Facel Vega. But beyond all this it had demonstrated the technique, and from henceforward the V8 became an ordinary engine form, to be used whenever power was a consideration. Up to the early '70s hardly a car was made in America that did not have a V8 power unit; and all because Henry Ford saw in it his way to beat the opposition.

The sign that made the name Ford synonymous with V8, and made the V8 idea, in the mind of the ordinary motorist, synonymous with Ford. It was not many months after its introduction, that a man could boast to his friends in the pub that he has just bought "a V8"– and no one was in any doubt that he meant a Ford.

When introduced in 1932 the cars carried bodies almost identical to those of the previous four cylinder models – and indeed a four cylinder range was offered at the same time. However, it was a giant step forward and dealers everywhere were urged to help with the initial publicity. Here a phaeton (tourer) has been given a plastic bonnet, so that around the town it became a mobile showroom. Note the V8 insignia on the hubcaps and on the tie-bar.

Almost as soon as the first V8 arrived on the British **market special**ist coachbuilders started making "sports cars" out of them. This is a "Greyhound" open four seater, before the start of the 1934 Monte Carlo rally (when open cars were not only allowed, but in favour). This redoubtable crew, J.A. Driskell, R. Silva, J. Walters and I. D. Stuthers, finished 62nd overall, but were the highest placed of all the John o'Groats starters.

The first V8s (model 18) were superceded after about a year by a much more handsome car – the model 40, seen here with Miss Finland 1934. This car has non-standard steel spoke wheels. The full blast of publicity was kept up through the announcement of this new model; but was allowed to cool somewhat after that, as the car had become established.

Although an inexpensive car the weight of public interest made it desirable for the rich as for anyone else; and not much prodding was required to make it clear for the Stars as well. Here is Joan Crawford, one of the great stars of the great days of Hollywood, in a 1934 model 40, specially created for her. With special wheels it was all white, even down to a white steering wheel and white leather upholstery. The greyhound mascot was a fairly usual extra copied from the Lincoln, Fords' prestige car.

Meanwhile the dealer's were still hard at it; and indeed the chassis alone made it clear what excellent value for money the company was offering. All sorts of regular accessories were also on offer, as for example the rear trunk which fitted neatly on to the back of the model 40 saloons, and seen here on the shelf (a similar style of thing was offered by Citroen in Europe).

The Ford V-8 was soon seen in competitions – here is a 1934 Model 40 roadster stripped for stock car racing, at a Californian dirt track.

One of 3 cars prepared for and run in the 1934 Ulster T.T. With bodies by Jensen complete with ultra large petrol tanks.

Stars were one thing, Royalty another; and in Great Britain there was no substitute for the Prince of Wales, who visited the Ford plant at Dagenham to see the new V8's being assembled. Cloth upholstery, now a commonplace, was not usual in British cars at the time but many of the early V8s had very simple but attractive grey cloth trim – and as grey went with almost any colour it was back to Henry Ford's old dictum "any colour you like as long as its black"– and in fact most of them were.

Open touring cars were still in vogue in the mid-thirties, and here is the Royal visitor going round the factory in one.

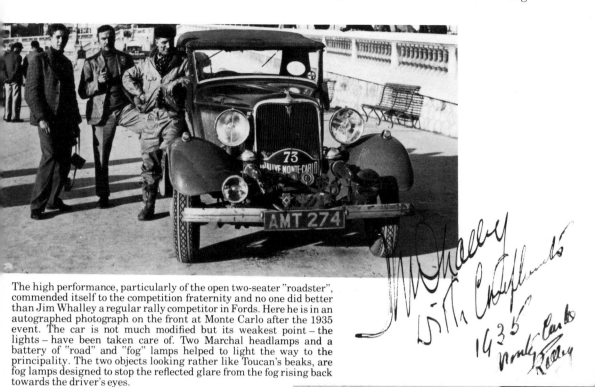

The high performance, particularly of the open two-seater "roadster", commended itself to the competition fraternity and no one did better than Jim Whalley a regular rally competitor in Fords. Here he is in an autographed photograph on the front at Monte Carlo after the 1935 event. The car is not much modified but its weakest point – the lights – have been taken care of. Two Marchal headlamps and a battery of "road" and "fog" lamps helped to light the way to the principality. The two objects looking rather like Toucan's beaks, are fog lamps designed to stop the reflected glare from the fog rising back towards the driver's eyes.

1936 was a bumper year for Ford in the Monte Carlo rally. Two cars which started from Athens made all the running, and most of the publicity. The slightly less extraordinary of the pair, driven by Zamfirescu and Cristea won the event; but the other driven by Colonel Berlescu was not in the money – he finished 19th. This latter car had a rounded bonnet like one of the contemporary Auto-Union Grand Prix cars, two very small seats and a pointed tail like a Bugatti. The actual "coachwork" however, was only made of doped canvas stretched over a frame in the manner of a light aeroplane. The other car, the winner, had at least the remains of a Ford roadster body. The doors were cut away and the spare wheels fitted just in front of the rear wings. It had a solid rear axle and the brakes were arranged in such a way that on full lock (either side) the front wheels ceased to revolve. (Anyone with experience of cable brakes of that time will know that the effect was all too easy to achieve without any special arrangements).

Neither of the cars did very well in their first runs over the notorious "wiggle-woggle"; but when it came to the second run, Cristea took over the Ford, and put up a performance for which it is said he had practised for literally months. He passed the first pylon flat out, spun the car completely, made a token reverse, shot off down the figure of eight – spinning the car again at the end of the test and finally crossed the line in 65 seconds dead to win the 15th Monte.

By 1935 a major change in shape became necessary, as the "streamline" fashion began to be felt, and the Model 48 was introduced. Some improvement in engine power matched the greater weight of the new cars, and though the smoothness remained, some of the edge had gone off the performance. These are convertible sedans – a relatively rare body style. Public acceptance was now complete; but other cars were catching up on performance and the Hudson and Terraplane models, for example, had as much performance to offer and at very nearly the same price; but they were not V8s and in that Ford held the market.

The Model 68 of the following year was little but a face lift of the front panels and radiator, though the wing line was also changed. Problems in marketing began to be evident in Great Britain where the cost of tax and petrol was high compared to America, and the low cost of buying a Ford V8 was contradicted by the high cost of running it. A man who could afford to run one, could usually afford to buy something much better in the first place; and no amount of annual model changing was going to get over that.

Ford therefore in 1936 introduced a British V8 called the 22 hp (the original American cars had been 30 hp by the old R.A.C. rating, on which tax was paid). In general terms the conception was the same but after a while a more European style was evolved. Though it cannot have cost much less to run than the larger cars, the idea of a "22" as against a "30" caught on with at least a section of the public; and the car's slightly smaller overall size made an appeal to some who thought the big car too big for their experience. American cars enjoyed a wide popularity in Great Britain at the time; but it was a love-hate relationship which must have given many a marketing man grey hairs. By 1938 the backend had been redesigned giving a small "boot" and considerably improving the appearance of the car, which had really begun to establish itself as the British V8; and it became more than ever true for the man in the street that V8 meant Ford V8.

Here are cars coming off the line at Dagenham in 1937 with a line of eights on the left of the picture. It is interesting to note that the third vehicle in the line is, in fact, a commercial so that the line was always mixed. On the radiator grille of the first car can be seen the more modern version of the V8 insignia, developed from the early design seen at the beginning of this section.

With mixed lines as the order of the day it is a little difficult in retrospect to know exactly what is going on. This is the Dagenham chassis line of 1936, the vehicle nearest the camera being a private car while the chassis in front, which does not have a transverse rear spring and does have four spokes to its steering wheel, is a commercial. The Ford V8 engine was already enjoying a very considerable success in the world of light vans and trucks, and making one engine for so many purposes obviously held down the ever rising costs.

The British 22 hp V8 body soon found its way into Europe, where Ford had set up a production line on the Mathis works – the cars produced being called Matfords. A rather more rakish front end was evidently considered necessary, and different lamps were fitted; but the chassis, engine and body were to all intents and purposes the same as the Dagenham cars. No reciprocal arrangements were made for the British to have what must have been one of the first "hatchbacks", produced by Matford in 1938. It is an interesting sidelight that the French hung the doors differently – the British have both doors front hinged and the French put both hinges on the centre pillar giving the less safe, but oh so much more practical, front opening.

Like its bigger brother the 22 hp model soon found its way into competition; but by far the most interesting thing in this picture is the weather, for despite the heavy snow it is not the 'Monte' but the R.A.C. Rally that is in question. The R.A.C. event in those days was a much tamer affair than it is now, but the snow would not have been welcome, to anyone but the organisers.

The vogue for the "Woodie", that is to say the wooden bodied estate car undoubtedly started in America, but spread quickly to this side of the Atlantic, where individual coachbuilders and carpenters could quickly and easily make individual models. Here is a 1937 Model. As well as a large capacity for goods the appeal of the "Woodie" was also its large family carrying capacity – and presumably the fact that it was a break away from the pressed steel box that had become a commonplace.

Here is a British 81A "Estate Car"– a rose by any other name. The expression "Woodie" did not come into Great Britain until after the war – or at least until after the education that the U.S. forces brought with them. The picture of the interior gives a good idea of the passenger space; but one must accept, in the context of this book, that a V8 engine was not strictly necessary.

Back to California where the snow comes in the dealer's showrooms (to help numb the senses to the small print in that awsome H.P. agreement?). Above the car hangs a lesson in Anglo-American nomenclature, for as you can see an Estate Car becomes a Station Wagon – Woodie is an affectionate, but later, label. This is a 1940 model.

Seen at Brooklands just before the outbreak of war is a 1939 Model 91A convertible cabriolet (in the background are two earlier models). Right to the end, the performance of the Ford V8 made it an interesting competition car, though the handling with those transverse springs both front and rear sometimes made it more interesting than the driver bargained for.

While a lot of enthusiasts took the performance of the newly introduced V8 as it stood – and made the most of it, others took the whole business more seriously. A young man by the name of Koppenhagen got hold of three of the early 1932 Model 18 cars – in their lightest two-seater form and in about 1936/7 put the latest version of the V8 engine in them. This had by then been made to produce an additional ten horse-power or so, and as he also cut down the wings, removed the running boards and generally lightened them, the performance really was electric. They ran as a team, often with "invited" drivers such as Gordon Wilkins, and had a brilliant competition record. Named the Jabberwocks after the poem in *Alice through the Looking Glass;*

"The Jabberwock with the eyes of flame
Came whiffling through the tulgey wood
and burbled as it came"

Which was a very fair description of one of the cars coming through a wood near dawn. In one of the then fashionable "reliability trials", one of the three cars is seen here in the 1937 M.C.C. Torquay Rally, followed by two of the 22 hp models.

On the other side of the Atlantic they also went to extremes; but not quite so successfully. Here is Ted Horn in a front drive Miller Special with a Ford V8 engine in it. It is doubtful if Harry Armenius Miller had much more to do with them than the front drive part, and they were always underpowered; but that anyone should even think of trying, is credit enough to this remarkable engine.

In 1933 Reid Railton had been commissioned to tidy up a Hudson chassis, and to lend his name to a range of cars with British coachwork based on the Hudsons mechanics. This set the fashion for Anglo-American cars where the cheap but powerful American power plants (and often chassis) were clothed in a shape more acceptable to European tastes – and the handling of the chassis was also suitably improved. Following Railton a Ford Dealer by the name of Allard made a trials special, pictured here. It was basically Ford V8 with the front transverse suspension system split to provide independence; and a light body (in this case off a Bugatti) fitted. It was given a distinctive radiator by the simple expedient of making a "stoneguard" of unusual shape to fit over the original Ford shell. Allard achieved considerable success with the car, and orders soon came for copies of it. A small series of production cars was put in hand (some using the side valve Lincoln Zephyr twelve cylinder engine – which was only a Ford V8 with four pots added) until after the war when he went into production on a much bigger scale; but still using the faithful old Ford V8

This is only the "artist's impression" of the production Allard – with Le Mans type body and no great provision, as far as one can see, for the driver and passenger to know where they were going.

This photo of the real thing, bears quite a striking resemblance to the advertisement.

Allard was not, of course, alone in his endeavours for here is a special built by R. E. Holt, seen here on Juniper, a well known trials hill, which amounted to much the same thing; but does serve to stress the universality of that Ford engine.

This is the Leidart, a car made in Pontefract, Yorkshire in very small numbers, looking rather like a blown-up Morgan. A saloon was advertised but no one seems to know if they made it or not. Similar in conception was another car called the Batten which was made in South London – and there were others.

The Continentals had a go too – this is the Edford made in Portugal from 1936 to 1938. It had coil independent front suspension, and an aluminium body which weighed only 150 kgs. The tuned engine was said to give a top speed of 110 mph.

Grand Prix driver Jean-Pierre Wimille was at work on this prototype in conjunction with Ford of France when he was killed in practice for the Buenos Aires Grand Prix in 1949. His original model had used Citroen Traction parts, but it had made such an impression that Ford France had taken it up. Sadly when he died Ford of Detroit not only refused to carry on with the idea, but forbade their French subsidiary to supply any further components – a strangely short-sighted action from the men who had succeeded a man with a sight long enough to risk his all on the V8.

Dick and Allan Jensen were brothers of Danish origin, but British birth, who had set up as coach designers and builders in the Midlands. They had a more than usual flair for design and this sports tourer, on a 1935 Model 48, was among their best. It is taking part in the 1938 Coventry Cup Trial organised by the N.W. London Motor Club. A similar car was supplied to Clark Gable in Hollywood.

Not content with their success with these open sports cars they set out to make a model of their own. Using their own chassis (some stories say it was a modified Ford truck chassis) and adding a two speed rear axle of Columbia design – similar to that fitted to the American Auburn they produced a "poor man's Bentley" of considerable attraction. Ford's approval was needed if supplies were to be maintained, and here are the Jensen brothers with Edsel Ford (in mack) and their new car.

A production example of the Ford V8-engined Jensen, of handsome appearance, good performance, silence and comfort it made an immediate appeal to those who wanted something different; but had some limit to the money at their disposal. This car is seen on the front at Blackpool having won an award in the 1938 R.A.C. Rally.

Then came the war. Ford like everyone else was turned over to making the tools of war, and the first Ford to go to the army was the 30 cwt truck as seen here. This was a fairly straightforward conversion from a vehicle already in production; beefed up in places and with a very simplified cab, wings and bonnet, it gave sterling service. Since its engine was used in so many other vehicles, spares were not difficult, cannibalisation being a quick answer when Army Form G 1098 proved unavailing.

This fire appliance is based on the military 15 cwt truck, a war-time botch up if ever there was one – though it worked perfectly well, from its V8 engine to its last war-time nut and bolt. The real problem was the war office requirement which had Ford make a miniature forward control job. This they did by putting the dashboard at the back of the engine, moving the steering forward, and accommodating the driver and passenger's legs in narrow tunnels between the engine and the wheel arches. Apart from anything else it made maintenance damn near impossible and even the army's famous W.O.F.L.T.B. (Water, Oil, Fuel, Lights, Tyres and Battery for those not old enough to remember) was not all that easily carried out. Worse still was the fact that there was not room in the tunnel on the driver's side for all three pedals – the clutch and the brake were alright, but the accelerator (hinged from the floor) had to be mounted *behind* the off side front wheel arch so that the driver had to have his right knee bent up towards his chest to operate it. With a rather sudden clutch (beefed up no doubt to deal with the load) and a biggish surge of power from the V8, starting off for the uninitiated (and many of the army drivers were just that – if not worse) was a hazardous and jumpy procedure. What Panhard said of the gearbox applied very well to the Truck W.D. 15 cwt – "its crude but it works".

Very soon came the demand for four-wheel-drive vehicles, and that ubiquitous V8 fitted that bill just as well – Ford's knowledge of mass production enabling them to turn out vast numbers of the things – and when you think they were making Rolls-Royce Merlin engines as well, imagination boggles . . .

This is General Alexander's desert staff car, an American rather than a European model – and probably built in Canada. In these conditions the good slogging power of the side-valve V8 was at its best.

Perhaps the most **famous war time role** of the Ford V8 was as the motive power for the "Bren Carrier". This fast, light, all purpose tracked vehicle, needed a good powerful engine of small dimensions with good torque; and the Ford V8 was ideal. Buried down in the inaccessible bowels of the machine it didn't need (and didn't get) much attention, and was happy to go on churning out its 70-odd bhp unendingly – and furthermore it was cheap to produce.

Several firms had made marine conversions of the Ford V8 for yachtsmen before the war; but few can have imagined it was going to power craft like this – a small personnel landing craft. Such was its versatility, that it became the natural choice.

Used in pairs – and sometimes as a triple installation, the old V8 did well in fast launches – the marine version usually being made out of what Ford liked to call their 'industrial' engine, which, before the end of its run, had powered just about everything on earth – but there is **no record** of its having taken to the air.

Taking to the air may be one thing; but taking to charcoal gas is another. However the undemanding nature of its low-compression, side-valve design, meant that when it came to the push you could run a V8 Ford truck on almost anything – and quite a number of people did. The gas was produced by passing air over burning charcoal, with a small quantity of steam being added.

Even if the army was asking for its own hybrids, the ordinary "run-of the-mill" Ford V8 van was still much in demand. Here, as a Y.M.C.A. dockland canteen.

And here with the N.F.S. (National Fire Service).

Whether the Assistance Board actually needed V8 power or not is a moot point; but it was one of the few available and serviceable trucks, so there was no end to the use that could be made of it. The picture proved nothing but the almost universal adaptability of Henry Ford's great step in making the V8 an everyday affair – a workhorse for the world, in peace and in war.

Came the peace and with it the need to get the swords back to ploughshears. Everyone was faced with making the cars they had before the war; but Ford were clever enough to gild the lily a little. They took the pre-war 22hp body shell, put the big V8 in it (they must have had hundreds lying about at the end of the war, and all the facilities for making hundreds more) and decorated the front with what one can only assume they felt to be a "British" look. Strange really since the pre-war V8s were already very up-to-date and streamlined. However, no doubt the marketing men knew which way to fly their Union Jacks; so, the Ford Pilot, as it was called, enjoyed its brief years of fame.

It made a nice powerful up-to-date "Woodie"; and this one, built for Princess Elizabeth, gave admirable service until replaced in the Royal Mews by one of the early Zephyr Sixes, which was still there up to a short while ago having done some quite prodigious mileage.

As the sun had not yet completely set on the British Empire, a lively export trade was looked for; and assisted in Uganda by a substantial order from the Police. What look like limousines, are probably all metal Estate cars. There is also a '46 Mercury in the line-up.

The Monte started again in 1949 and there was still enough urge in a Ford V8 to make it an interesting proposition in this hazardous event. Number 221 seen at the finish is that of Westwood and Austin, and number 238 rounding the "Gas Works" hairpin in one of the eliminating tests is driven by White and Brown, both in 1951. A similar car driven by Ken Wharton and J. Langelaan finished joint 6th overall.

And while the motorist was trying to get back to normal so was commerce, and the faithful V8 which had served so many men so very well during the war, was a natural choice for many who needed vehicles for their peace-time work. Here are two examples from the "Thames" range; but by now the writing was on the wall, and the drawing offices of Dearborn and Dagenham were busy with other designs to replace the famous V8. There would be fours and sixes and some V8s of a different breed;but the break through of 1932 had run its course, and after some twenty years was to make way for new developments.

CHAPTER THREE

As A Matter of Course

Up to the outbreak of the Second World War almost everyone, from California to New York, or Constantinople to Old York, was happy enough driving about behind a side-valve engine. Most people found them more than adequate; and if at any given time more power was needed, designers, particularly American ones, found that they only had to add a few litres. Of course students of engineering and anyone familiar with Pomeroy's famous book "The Grand Prix Car" will know that a certain Mr Henry, together with the drivers Zucarelli, Goux and Boillot got interested in twin overhead camshafts; and even if historians are still debating who exactly should get the credit, the fact remains that they opened, in the Grand Prix Peugeot, a new avenue to power. Some many years later in the twenties and thirties, Georges Roesch, the Swiss designer of the British Talbots, did wonders with push-rods, though nobody made nearly so much fuss about him; but for all these efforts the world and his wife were happy with their reliable side-valve machines, which chugged happily on.

Developments in aircraft engines, in metallurgy, and know how, some modifications to the tax systems in various countries, and other external forces during and after the second world war, made the use of over-head valves (camshaft or push-rod) the accepted thing when peace returned. For a short while the V8 Ford went on; but after a few years it, and the other side-valve engines, were on the shelf.

In 1949 Cadillac, who had remained great exponents of the V8, came out with an ohv, high compression V8 engine in the newly fashionable "square" design with bore and stroke being near equal. It was not revolutionary in itself, but it did revolutionise American thinking; and everyone followed suit, so that almost every American car, save the cheapest, had a push-rod operated ohv V8 engine for its power. And as time went on such engines became if anything almost more universal. Europe went a different way, the greater available power for a given engine size made for smaller lighter cars; and, as in America before the war, only the largest and most luxurious, Rolls-Royce and Mercedes-Benz for example, went to big V8 engines.

The paradox is that in America, where overall speed restriction came much sooner than in Europe, there was a mad race for power; though this was directed more towards acceleration than straight line speed, and engines of over two hundred horsepower became a commonplace in cars not officially supposed to exceed 50 mph on the highway. The peak of the power race was in the Chrysler "Hemi" a push-rod V8 with hemispherical cylinder heads (hence its nickname) which came in 1951. Almost as suddenly as the great race for power started, it stopped; but the V8 remained the all American choice.

The last facet in the story is, of course, allied to racing. When the new 3-litre Grand Prix formula was introduced, Ford, not unassisted by a certain Mr Duckworth, set about making their second world-beating V8, and after its first victory in the Dutch Grand Prix of 1967 the Ford DFV Grand Prix engine has not looked back. It has further gone some way to prove that eight cylinders in a V formation are enough, and that the twelves can be no better. Most engineers would say this was not entirely true, but only Ferrari so far have come anywhere near proving it. There were, of course, other racing V8s as well from Brabham, BRM and others; while outside the Grand Prix world, Ford developed V8 engines to win both Indianapolis and Le Mans.

Now the time has come when they may be on the wane, for they are usually big and do tend to guzzle fuel – and that is no longer an acceptable trait; but until governments and common sense finally get the better of us, that distinctive burble may yet contrive to gladden our ears.

With the war out of the way Sydney Allard went back into production with his Ford V8-engined cars in a much bigger way. Indeed, he was not only one of the "new" manufacturers, but also in the years after the war one of the most prolific. Being a small company producing a specialist car, it was perhaps easier for him to get going than it was for some of the larger manufacturers. At all events, he enjoyed a very rapid rise to fame, and with his competition background it was obviously not long before his mind got back on that track. The original two-seater was much modified, and became a very fast car indeed. The British versions had, after a short while, o.h.v. conversions to the old Ford V8 (which was getting a bit long in the tooth), but cars for America were powered with the new big American o.h.v. V8s such as the Cadillac seen here. Allard himself put up a good show at Le Mans, and won the Monte Carlo Rally in one of the saloons in 1952.

L- type sports tourer indulges in some active cornering during the London Motor Club's Little Rally in April, 1953. P.1 Saloon on the starting line at a Brunton Hill Climb. A later standard drop-head coupé in repose.

A useful link between the old Ford V8 and all the cars that followed from it is the French Ford Comète which first became available in 1952. The post-war French Fords used the old side-valve V8, in its smallest version, in a much more modern chassis based on the current American design. The introduction of the Comète which had a body by Facel led indirectly to the famous Facel Vega – one of the most ambitious of the many European cars to use American engines. This effort in France, together with the Pilot in Great Britain was the swan song of the old V8; and the battle for more power with higher octane petrol was soon to banish the side-valve engine, for all its simple merits. It is worth noting that most Comètes were fixed-head coupés, and very few of this convertible model were made.

It would be a good deal less than fair to call the Ford Comète a sow's ear; but you certainly needed a silk purse to run a Facel Vega, which was its logical successor. The Facel company started out as body builders to the industry, and worked in that capacity for Panhard, Simca and Ford. When they decided to go into the French luxury market, to fill the gap left by the demise of Talbot, Delahaye, Delage and Hotchkiss, they produced a handsome coupé powered by the Chrysler "Hemi" in its 4.5 litre version – this was in 1954. Later they fitted bigger engines and in 1958 they produced a four-door version. The last of the coupés – more handsome than this one – had 6.3 litre engines giving 390bhp and a top speed of about 145mph; which was a bit faster than most of the owners, or the design of the chassis, could cope with.

It was a mad world just after the war – and some of the madness happily persisted on into the beginning of the fifties. In 1951 the Empresa Nacional de Autocamiones – that is to say the National Lorry-building Co. – of Barcelona decided to go into the car market in no small way. Using what had been the training department of the old Hispano-Suiza works they got Wilfredo Ricart to design a 2½ litre V8 sports car. They made only the chassis, in the best pre-war tradition, and some very exotic bodies appeared as the French coachbuilding industry was in its death throes. This two-seater by Saoutchik, always the most exotic and often the most vulgar of all the French greats has real flair – the real problem of the car is best summed up in what someone said about Bugattis many many years before – "the car is not very reliable, so you don't motor very often – but by God when you do . . . ." Sadly this splendid argument did not go down too well in the showrooms, and the cars (there were several different models) went out of production in favour of trucks.

And here are the heady delights of that splendid design, laid bare at the Paris show for even the police to enthuse over. Called the Pegaso, it was indeed a horse with wings; but one which sadly never took off in marketing terms. Only about 125 were made, and their competition successes were few or they might well have become a challenge to the Italian super sports cars. Now they should become something for collectors to collect, and a new fame may be coming their way.

From the time Cesare Isotta and Vincenzo Fraschini had shaken off their many outside associations and settled down after World War One to make big luxury cars for the American market, they were wedded to a one model straight eight car. After the second war, the pre-war model, which was already pretty long in the tooth, would not serve, and a new design had to be embarked upon. The Monterosa shown here was a rear engined V8 of 3.4 litres with a single overhead camshaft to each block. It had a five speed gearbox and a strong chassis for the Italian coachbuilders of the time to work on. There was a catalogue of splendid designs, few of which ever left the paper they were conceived on, and in all only six were made. None were conventionally sold though some, one supposes must in the end have got into private hands. The company folded in 1949.

With rear engines and powerful ones at that already on our minds it is a good moment to have another look at the Tatra we saw in Chapter One. In basic conception it has changed very little, and only the most recent models have done away with the streamlined "tail" and replaced it by something much nearer the Isotta we have just looked at. It has been tidied up; and, with all that space around it, this is one V8 that is not difficult to work on. The space is very necessary as the car is air cooled – the tops of its two cooling fans can just be seen above the rear sill.

In no circumstances must you call this a V8, for though it has eight cylinders in a V formation its makers, the illustrious Fiat organisation, insisted that it be called an "8V". There is a story that Ford had some kind of copyright over the words "V8" – certainly they had a registered trade mark with the eight inside the V; but how much further their domain could extend over common usage is not quite clear. Anyhow to avoid confusion in the "F" section of any list of cars, Fiat decided on the opposite. The car came out in 1952 and was a rather unlovely, but very quick, two litre sports coupé capable of about 120mph. It certainly gave a lift to the rather prosaic post-war image the Italian giant had developed.

Meanwhile all those rich Americans were making rich V8s of enormous power, for very little money. Their expertise in mass production had been developed to a point where the finest tolerances were possible with very little hand work indeed; and in the resulting power race the Chrysler "Hemi" was introduced. It gave the bulbous and unlovely American sedan a turn of speed almost beyond belief, and that notable Belgian journalist and racing driver, Paul Frere, entered one in the 1953 Mille Miglia.

For a brief but splendid spell after the second war, when racing was again the name of the game, the French Talbot company, now under command of Major Anthony Lago, once the proud owner of a second-hand car site opposite the Kilburn Empire, and more recently the European Concessionaire for Wilson Gearboxes, had proved how successful an unblown 4½ litre car could be against the more potent 1½ litre supercharged models. They lasted longer, and there were many races in which lasting meant winning. Sadly, for all the splendours of their efforts, the French tax man made the production of big expensive sports cars and their attendant "exterior signs of richness" (signes extérieurs de la richesse) something that even the best heeled French were not prepared to show. Tony Lago tried hard to keep pace with the times and to expand his overseas markets; and this lovely little coupé with its 2½ litre V8 BMW engine was near the end of the story. Shortly after this the clock struck twelve and the last belle of the French industry left the party in a hurry.

Dick and Alan Jensen first became motor manufacturers with the Ford V8-engined cars that were in the last chapter. After the war, the old side-valve V8 would not do, and the British Government in its wisdom (or lack of it) hedged industry about with so many import restrictions that the post-war Jensens had to make do with Austin engines – and they did very well. However by 1963 the restrictions had been eased, and the need for a faster and more powerful car was being felt. They therefore revised the last of the Austin-engined sixes, and made the CV8 – naming it after its power unit, that redoubtable Chrysler "Hemi" – only they got theirs from the marine division; but it came to the same thing. The car had a glass-fibre body, very interesting trim, and seats which could be adjusted in the small of the driver's back to suit individual tastes. A first-aid kit was standard. If the appearance seemed a little odd at the time, those headlamps for example, then history is on the side of the Jensen brothers, for it looks better now than it did when it was new!

Jensen's biggest moment was the decision to join with the Fergusson organisation in making the Four-Wheel-Drive Jensen FF. Fitted with Dunlop "maxaret" breaking, and constant Four-Wheel-Drive, the Jensen must have been one of the safest handling cars ever – and it will no doubt become a collector's piece of great importance. It can be distinguished from the more usual models by the double line of vents towards the rear of the engine compartment; the other cars, which have shorter bonnets, have only one.

Not far removed from the Jensen in spirit is the Gordon Keeble built round a Chevrolet engine, instead of the Chrysler used by Jensen. The car was the work of Jim Keeble, whose partner John Gordon had previously made some interesting coupés based on Triumph T.R. components. Sadly the Gordon Keeble company had a very up and down life, changing hands many times before it finally expired, and a good car was lost. The car, which was made with ordinary manual transmission, could boast of the heaviest clutch ever presented to a driver's left foot – it was not, therefore, a car for London. However, once on the open road, it was a particularly splendid "Grand Tourer".

The ultimate accolade for splendour (outside Rolls-Royce) should perhaps go to the Bristol, which started life as an offshoot of the Bristol Aeroplane Company, and used a re-hash of the pre-war BMW engine. Later Anthony Crook and his partners bought the company from Bristols when the government were re-shaping the British Aero industry; and the more recent cars have been fitted with Chrysler engines not unlike the one used in the Jensen – his is a 1962, "407". Production has always been very small, and very special; and there are probably very few cars in the world as well built as a Bristol.

The old formula in a new guise – another British sports car fitted with a Ford V8 engine. This time, of course with an o.h.v. Ford V8. A.C. cars of Thames Ditton have a long tradition of making light cars, many of them with sporting pretensions; indeed the first British win in the Monte Carlo Rally won by the Hon. Victor Bruce driving an A.C. In the years after the war they developed, on a chassis designed by Tojeiro, an open sports two seater called the "Ace", at first with their own A.C. engine, and then powered by the Bristol. Since it was easy to fit any power unit into that frame some cars were made with the alternative of a Ford Zephyr – and then egged on by Carroll Shelby in America – they went for real power in one of the big o.h.v. Ford V8s – the car seen here racing at Snetterton is just such a model, now called the A.C. Cobra, and one of the most exciting sports cars ever made.

After the success of the Cobra; and with export markets in mind AC produced then own luxury coupé with British chassis, American engine (Ford) and Italian body (Frua). A rag top was also available.

A similar train of thought brought about the Sunbeam "Tiger". The car was invented by Norman Garrard's son, who was living in California at the time, and had the idea of squeezing a Ford V8 into the Sunbeam Alpine chassis. It all went so well that Rootes decided to take it up, and the car was put into production using the name "Tiger" which had been one of the most successful of the inter-war Sunbeam racing cars. As there was no facility for such production in the Rootes Group itself, Jensen in fact built the cars. When Chrysler came along and bought the company, it was found that the Chrysler V8 would not go into the space available, and as Chrysler could hardly be expected to build a Ford the project came to an earlier end than might otherwise have been the case. It was a very fast, very civilised car that went like a rocket.

So much so that the police became interested in it as a chase car; and here is one outside the old New Scotland Yard buildings on the Embankment, with Chief Supt. R. Butler, Commander N. Radford and Assistant Commissioner A. G. P. Way behind the car.

The business of cramming a big American engine into a lively European chassis was not unique to Great Britain – or at least not after the continentals had got hold of the idea. One of the more interesting cars was the Iso Rivolta, which, like the Gordon Keeble, used a Chevrolet engine. It could manage 0-60 in 7.9 seconds and 0-100 in only 20; and this for 1966 was good going.

If the Americans seem to have made most of the running in the development of post war V8s it is probably because larger engines were the order of the day across the Atlantic, whereas in Europe the post war recovery called for smaller units; and the V8 configuration lends itself to the bigger capacities. However, there was one man who made considerable progress on this side of the water and that was Edward Turner, chiefly remembered for his Triumph Motor Cycle engines. He designed for Daimler a range of V8s that are now coming to be remembered as remarkably fine units. Among the cars built with these engines was the Daimler "Dart" or SP 250 – a sports car with a glass-fibre body and pretty awful looks. However, such were the merits of the car, that it enjoyed quite a success in its day (this picture is October 1962) and now the cars are fast becoming collectors' pieces.

When Jaguar took over the Daimler Company, one of the first things they did was put the SP 250 engine into a Mark II Jaguar saloon – re-design the Jaguar front with flutes, to give a Daimler image; and, hey-presto, the new 2½ litre Daimler V8 saloon was on the market.

Much more Daimler; but using a larger version (4 litre) of the same design was the big Majestic Major Saloon. Much overlooked in its day, and even now not a sought-after car, the day will probably come when its virtues are recognised. Then, if there are any left, they will be interesting cars indeed. This particular car, recognisable by its number plate, was the property of Lord Brabazon of Tara – pioneer motorist and airman.

An interesting hybrid is this Daimler V8-powered Ogle SX 250 also made in '62; and whose shape eventually found its way into the Reliant Scimitar Saloon, where unfortunately the V8 engine did not follow it.

It would be nice, at all events for the British, to think that the Rover V8 was a truly national creation. Sadly, the truth is that the basic design is from General Motors (the Buick and Pontiac divisions) and that much as it may have been improved upon, and anglicised, it is really another of those American V8s. Unusual in its use of aluminium it is lighter than most of its contemporaries; and, as developed by Rover, a very striking power unit indeed, which probably still has a long life in front of it.

Besides finding a place in what had been the 2000 shell, the V8 was also put into the old 'up-market' three-litre, to give it a further lease of life. For many diehards this was the last of the "Rover" Rovers; and good as the present cars may be, and glad as some are to have lost the "aunty" image, when nostalgia is guiding the conversation, this is what Rover really means.

When nostalgia is not guiding the conversation the SD I is the Rover of the moment, as well as having been the "Car of the Year". Owing a good deal to Pininfarina in shape, and GM in engine, it is perhaps more worthy than inspired; but as an essay in motoring in the 1970s it has enjoyed, and will no doubt continue to enjoy, very notable success.

Designed before the Leyland mergers could have their full effect comes the Triumph Stag (which would surely otherwise have had the Rover engine in it). This V8 is in effect two of the blocks originally designed (and for a while made) by Triumph for Saab, mounted on a common crankcase. A fine powerful unit it seems a shame that it was never found useful outside the limited production of the Stag, and already out of production.

Far from out of production, even if to some eyes long out of date, is the Morgan; now available with the Rover V8 to give it the massive performance present day enthusiasts demand.

The ultimate accolade for the V8 configuration was its adoption by Rolls-Royce with the introduction of the Silver Cloud III. All his life Henry Royce had been a V12 man, in aero engines and in the Phantom III, which incidentally came but two years after his death. Perhaps it was felt that the V12 would have been a bit too much in these post war years; but whatever the cause, Rolls-Royce made their second V8 – their first being the second car in this book. While being a typical Rolls-Royce unit, it has all the overtones of the post war American developments; and even a Rolls-Royce trained chauffeur will find changing the plugs on a Silver Cloud III a good deal less convenient than on a Silver Cloud II – so much for progress.

Probably still the best, and outside one-off specials certainly the most expensive car in the world, the RR Camargue also, of course, uses a V8 engine.

Meanwhile, back on the mainland of Europe, the pencils were busy on the drawing boards as engineering fashion moved the V8 way – and this 1964 A.T.S. from Italy was one of the products. With a small 2½ litre V8 amidships this retains all the Italian dash one would expect, and uses the V8 to good purpose giving a lot of power and taking little space.

Generally regarded as a flop as far as sales were concerned, the Quattroporte Maserati was, as its name implied, the first car with more than two doors ever to leave the Maserati factory. Fitted with a big V8 engine it was said to do more than 140 mph "with all the comfort of a limousine"– perhaps that is just what prospective Maserati owners didn't want!

One of the lesser known Europeans was the V8 Glas. BMW took the firm over just about the time this picture was taken so its future was very limited; but it was a good looker and at 2.6 litres one of the smallest V8s in overall size, which may have hindered rather than helped it.

Back to the "brute force and bloody ignorance" school, this 1966 V8 Bizzarrini GT 500 used a 5½ litre V8 Chevvy engine with a De Dion back axle – over 160 mph was claimed. Bizzarrini had designed the Iso Grifo, and the car shown here is a similar conception.

A few years later the same company had gone into cahoots with Giugiaro of Ital Design to produce a really striking car called the Manta – the only trouble being that no one was quite sure if the engine was in it or not; but it would be safe to presume a V8 was intended. This was just the kind of design exercise for which the Turin show is noted; and in a world where new models are few and far between, and are all beginning to look exactly the same anyway, this is something to be thankful for.

Alfa Romeo first produced the Montreal as an exhibition piece for the town of that name – it then burst upon the European Market at Geneva, and heralded Alfa's return to the grand manner after some years of making family boxes (good, special family boxes if you like, but family boxes just the same). The styling here is by Bertone whose rapid rise to fame after the second world war brought the company into a position of being the only real competition for Pininfarina. After all those lovely straight eights before the war, the V8 seems somehow ordinary; but no Alfa Romeo engine was ever quite ordinary, so we must accept the change in fashion.

Once there was a good V8 in the offing from Alfa, it did not take long for it to appear in competition guise. This time the clothes are from Pininfarina.

For all their efforts with engines of their own, the Italians were never far from the idea of the big American "muscle" engine; and here is another example, the De Tomaso Mangusta which had a Ford unit.

And so back to the United States where the V8 has
made its natural home, but where the occasional
European flourish is often welcome. This is a 1949
Cadillac, from the era when the new and powerful
o.h.v. V8s were just getting under way. The coachwork
is by the most flamboyant of French coachbuilders,
Saoutchik, with great chromium splashes on the wings
in his typical manner, and with painted canework on
the doors just to show that it could still be done.
Saoutchik went on just into the fifties, as the last of the
great French coachbuilders. Always a little vulgar but
never less than interesting, this, one of his last cars,
begins to forge the link between America and Europe,
that was to be fostered from both sides of the Atlantic
in the ensuing years – particularly with the up and
coming Italian coachbuilders.

In pure American terms this 1949 Mercury (a Ford V8
by any other name) is typical of the bulbous post war
styling.

These two cars, both V8s, make an interesting contrast
in styling. The old car is a 1929/30 Lincoln, a *marque*
still with us. The more modern car is a 1953 Packard
Caribbean, whose manufacturers for all their pre-war
prestige, have now gone to the wall – their ghosts
remaining on the files of American Motors.

Back in the "bulge" period, this is the '51 Oldsmobile. This division of General Motors was prominent in the development of powerful V8s in the early fifties, and though such cars were somewhat despised in Europe, no one should forget that their performance was truly remarkable. Maybe they didn't steer, maybe they didn't stop, but they went like rockets (which was incidentally an Oldsmobile model name).

If the Europeans were busy importing American engines, some of the Americans were busy importing European bodies – and European chassis conceptions. One of these was millionaire Briggs Cunningham, who started making cars bearing his name in small numbers. This 1952 model has Vignale coachwork and a Chrysler engine. Cunningham made a determined assault on Le Mans in the years just after the war, as you can see in the racing section which follows this.

The Famous Ford Thunderbird before it was allowed to grow and grow beastly. Here from 1955 is one of the original "T-Birds" in all its glory. With a big powerful V8 it got as near as anything in America ever got to being a real sports car. Its great rival was the Chevrolet Corvette (this is a 1956 model) of which all the same things could be said – save that when the Corvette grew up it managed to retain much of its original character.

Going back a bit in time this is the '51 Chrysler Imperial. Important because in the power race which developed inside the widening use of o.h.v. V8 engines, the Chrysler "Hemi" (because it had hemispherical cylinder heads) was the leader. One of the most sophisticated and powerful production engines ever made, it is without question one of the great landmarks in the V8 story.

Over the years Chrysler developed a fine range of big cars which were unashamedly sold on their sheer power. With an overall maximum speed limit in many places one wonders how they managed to sell them on their native market. The Grand Prix of the Traffic Lights can hardly be the only answer – perhaps it was just a love of power. In which case when we come to ponder upon their ultimate demise, we ought to remember the words of Lord Acton "Power corrupts, and absolute power corrupts absolutely."

And some of the corruption was to be seen in American design generally during this period. Good as the engineering may have been, and masterly as the mass production undoubtedly was, the shapes were psychologists nightmares of sexual inhibitions (or at least so the psychologists tell us). Looking at the front end of this 1956 De Soto (one of Chrysler's sub makes) readers can decide for themselves "who does what and with which and to whom"– all we need add is, that it does it with a V8 engine!

But in the middle of it all there were some American designers and some American manufacturers who made a real effort to produce something much better. This is a Studebaker designed by Raymond Loewy. His original sloping front has given way to a sort of "radiator"; but the overall impression is still good – and the engine still a V8.

There is nothing to add to this picture save that it confirms the psychologists foreboding from the De Soto we have just seen – this being the back end of a Dodge (also a Chrysler sub make). It also confirms that V8 was still something to write on the boot lid, even if it had long ceased to be anything to write home about.

The unhappy Edsel – Ford's foray into the fantastic, named after the company's second boss – and, of course, fitted with a V8 engine. Ford spent a fortune on the launch of this car, and as much time and energy as only they could spend on the market research and development of it. Why it mis-fired is anyone's guess – the odd "horse-collar" radiator may not have helped; but it looked less odd in its day than it does now.

The ultimate in Chrysler Power was the "300" series – and here are the works of the 1961 car. Every available inch of space under that vast bonnet (or hood as the Americans would have it) is put to full use.

Here is Studebaker again with further variations on the original design; and just before the company moved to Canada on the way to giving up. They had already merged with Packard; but despite the quality of the cars they made, there was no place for them in the market.

And here from a few years before the final collapse is a Packard Clipper (note the ships' wheel in the middle of the grille). One of the factors that led to so many of the smaller U.S. manufacturers going out of business was the prodigious cost of new models and new engines. In earlier times, when cars had been less massed produced, the smaller firms could keep up; but by the end of the fifties this had become impossible, and defeat stared many of them in the face.

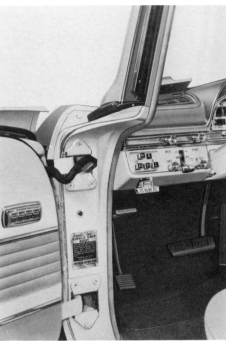

As with the whole history of American automobile engineering so with the V8 – the watchword is convention. Nothing outlandish; but good common sense and common practice allied to very fine tolerances by automated methods, have made the modern engine what it is – powerful and reliable, if a little thirsty. This is the 1958 Rambler Ambassador.

For those unfamiliar with the controls of more modern Americans this may come as something of a revelation – again this is the Rambler Ambassador. Push buttons on the left operate the automatic transmission (a Chrysler unit in this case) with N.R. D1. D2. and L (for low) giving control by choice of any of the ratios and neutral The "Park" lever under the buttons, gives the P position we are used to seeing on our quadrants. Below is the parking brake release, and below that the parking brake pedal – which stays down against a ratchet until released by the lever. It works well enough with automatic transmission. The main brake pedal can be seen clearly marked "Power Brake" and way over almost out of shot is the big organ type accelerator. The cable to the door provides for the electric window operation: all four windows being controllable from this, the driver's door.

Getting much nearer today the 1964 Pontiac Bonneville convertible which shows how American design tendencies have "slowed down" over the recent years; and change for the sake of change is beginning to go out of fashion. Sadly the convertible was also going out of fashion, in America as in Europe, and while the sun still shines one is forced to wonder why.

One of the major steps taken by the American industry in recent years was the Oldsmobile Toronado. A V8 powered front-wheel-drive concept going back, if you like, to the great days of Cord. Certainly the largest and most powerful f.w.d. car ever to be put on the market, it was something like an instant success. And by any standards it was good looking despite the excessive front overhang.

Two 1971 Cadillacs, the convertible in the foreground being the "Eldorado". In fact the same front-wheel-drive concept as the Toronado. Behind is the more conventional, but still of course V8, Fleetwood Sedan de Ville.

If you want to know in full measure just how far apart the American and European markets are, you can do no better than read the caption to this photograph, as supplied by the Lincoln-Mercury Public Relations Department, which reads:–"Significant power-team changes, new front and rear appearances, an upgraded series and many new options highlight the 1974 Mercury Montego line. The 302-c.i.d. 2V V8 becomes the standard engine on all Montego models and SelectShift automatic transmission is now standard on all station wagons. The powerful 460 c.i.d. 4V V8 is a new option on all 1974 Montego models. Additions to Montego's already extensive option list are new Custom trims for the MX Brougham and Villager models, opera windows and Embassy vinyl roof for two-door hardtops, a speed-control system and an AM/FM/MPX stereo radio system with tape player." Not the sort of thing you get with a Morris Marina.

The 1977/8 Cadillac Fleetwood Brougham – not really so good looking as the 1971 car – but to go with it they also produce the Seville, which is smaller and neater.

Despite the bad quality of the picture one might easily be forgiven for thinking this to be an early post war Packard. Of course it is not, being in fact the Russian copy, the Zil III from 1959. As well as the shape the Russians copied the engine – a V8.

Looking more like the work of a north-country specialist coachbuilder to the funeral trade, this is in fact the largest car made in Japan in the 1960s. The Nissan Prince Royal was a one-off built for the Emperor, using the 4 litre 180 bhp V8 engine of the Nissan President with a considerably extended wheelbase.

Somehow one does not look to America for automobile eccentricity, yet it persists there as elsewhere, with the added interest, as far as this book is concerned, that it usually has a V8 engine. This extraordinary contraption is called the "Ostentatienne Opera Sedan" (quite why Americans always confuse their cars with opera houses is a fact yet to be explained). It was designed by Bruce Baldwin Mohs and its main concern was with safety. To this end it had no doors at the side, entry being up the ramp at the back, and its seats which "swung laterally" (and sickeningly?) on corners, also pivoted back to a horizontal position in the case of a head on collision! About four of them were made at a cost of about $20,000 each fitted with the smaller of the several engine options, a 250 bhp 4,976 cc V8. The front end is a kind of nightmare Rolls-Royce, and the curious wheels have flying eagles girating unhappily around the centres. It dates from 1968.

Much more seriously interesting is the work of the more important individual stylists in America, Brooks Stevens being among the best. This is an early effort in 1954 called the Cadillac Valkyrie – first shown at the Paris show that year, with its body built by the famous German coachbuilder Spohn of Ravensburg. For us the prominence of the V8 symbol on the front of the car is significant – for the rest it is an effort to break with tradition without being outlandish and is full of little design details that others were later to copy.

Arising almost directly out of the Valkyrie is another Brooks Stevens effort, the Gaylord. This used Chrysler running units and was intended as a serious production car by its makers Gaylord Motor Car Co. of Chicago, Illinois. A two-seater – model name "Gentleman"– like the Valkyrie it had its body built by Spohn. Sadly at $10,000 there were not enough takers for it to survive.

Survival is the name of the game with these "specialist" efforts – most of which use regular engines and running units anyway. This is the Stutz – an effort to cash in on a famous name of the past, to provide something different for today. Designed by Virgil Exner, one time head of styling at Chrysler, it employs Pontiac running units along with the V8 engine. Quite prodigious in price and exquisitely vulgar in its trimmings (although the overall conception is pleasantly nostalgic) it is still in production, appearing again in 1978 at the Turin show (it was launched in 1971). Pop stars, oil magnates, and others to whom ostentation is not anathema, will doubtless keep it ticking over – and the design is at least fairly timeless. The bodies are built by the Italian firm, Carrozzeria Padana.

Back to Brooks Stevens and what the Americans are apt to call the 'Replicar' business. If you are not revolted by the very idea of a "copy" then at least this effort to reproduce the glories of the SSK Mercedes, without the attendant mechanical problems, is not without authenticity. The Excalibur SS as it was called first appeared about 1966 which is the car shown here (it later developed a much less happy four seater). It does have its own chassis (to house an American V8 of course) and the 1970 version of that, Excalibur Series II, is also shown.

Once you start cramming V8 engines of proprietry manufacture into other chassis there is almost no end to the possible variations. Here, the humble model T Ford, is what naturalists would probably call the 'host'. Hot rods in which power is the essential element have all too often not much place to keep it, and the V8 engine, especially in its American post war form, was the obvious solution. This is from the film "Teen Age Thunder"– a reminder that the distinctive thunder of the V8 has been with us since near the dawn of motoring; and although nowadays it is more often than not reduced to a burble the sound is still a distinctive and distinguishing feature of the engine.

CHAPTER FOUR

Ford V8 - the Second Coming

If the original Ford V8 became the workhorse of the world, it would be fair to suggest that the second Ford V8 became the racehorse of the world. Not that there had been any shortage of V8s in the racing scene before the Ford Cosworth DFV engine appeared; and there are some of them on the ensuing pages. All the same, in recent years one could say with some truth, that the second Ford V8 has totally dominated the Grand Prix scene for the past several years – and looks like going on in the same vein for some time.

For generations racing had been given over, as far as eight cylinder cars were concerned, to the straight eight – one of the best balanced and most aesthetically pleasing of all engine configurations. There is nothing, and will never be anything, quite the equal of Bugatti or Alfa Romeo or Miller in this field; and for all the twelves and sixteens of the Hitler teams, and all the Ferraris and Lamborghinis ever made, those straight

eights remain one of the highlights of motoring history.

But times change and after the war, when money was tight and racing difficult, someone put a motor bike engine behind the driver in a tiny racing car and made the first Formula III (or 500 formula as it was usually called). Soon someone tried putting a 1000cc V twin in the back and going after the bigger cars – then came a four cylinder, and the shape of the racing car had changed. Yes, we know all about the Auto Union growing out of Dr. Rumpler; but the fact remains that the present Grand Prix car grew out of a 500, much more than out of the Auto Union, which was quite a different conception.

No longer was there any room for straight eights, and the V8 became the obvious solution; and so we can come, at the end of this book, to a generation of V8 racers – dominated, as the V8 scene has always been, by Ford.

June 1966 and after some years of effort the three Ford II-A sports-prototypes cross the finishing line at Le Mans to record the first American victory in this classic race – with V8 engines, of course.

It is surprising how often the same names crop up in the V8 story, and Sydney Allard, as one of the great individualists of the industry, must necessarily be one of them. We have observed elsewhere in the book how the post war two seater was quickly developed into a competition car – well here it is at Brighton Speed Trials, in September 1950, setting a new sports car record with none other than Sydney Allard himself at the wheel. Some measure of its performance can be gained by the fact that the cars are barely away from the start – and just look what it is doing to an XK Jaguar.

The Cadillac-engined J2 in which Sydney Allard (at the wheel) and Tom Cole finished 3rd at Le Mans in 1950. This was the make's best placing at the famous 24 hour event.

Even more individual was Sid Allard's hillclimb special, seen here at Shelsley Walsh in 1949. Although the radiator cowl, wheels, and other parts are from the production Allard (with an eye to publicity no doubt), the engine is an air cooled war time Steyr V8, which featured in a number of the Wehrmacht's desert vehicles, and was fairly easy to come by in the first days of peace. Allard made it go; and the light weight must have helped.

Another great individualist was Briggs Cunningham, whose name has also appeared elsewhere in this book. Here he is at Le Mans in 1953 with one of the Chrysler V8-engined Cunninghams built for the race. Although victory was denied them, they finished 3rd, 7th and 10th; and in the second picture Briggs Cunningham himself, with suitably attractive standard bearer, brings in No. 1, which finished third.

It is one thing to be a rugged individual in the sports car world; but it takes an Australian of Jack Brabham's quality to go for the top in Grand Prix racing – and make it. As soon as the three litre formula came into operation there was a general state of panic – for no one seemed ready for it. But without any fuss at all, Jack Brabham had gone off home to the other side of the world, and come back with his own new engine.

Assisted by the Australian Repco company he had made, on the basic block of the General Motors aluminium V8 (which now in a different guise powers the Rover) a Grand Prix engine of note. They had worked fast and economically, using, for example, the con-rods from a production Daimler at a few quid a set.

With a new neat chassis, Brabham the man, and Brabham the car, made rings round the Grand Prix scene for at least one glorious season.

An interesting spin-off from the Brabham Grand Prix cars was the use by Frank Matich – five time Australian Sports Car Champion – of the Repco engine in his 1969 Matich-Repco sports car. Matich started out with his own re-worked version of the Lotus 19 chassis, into which he had put a Travis and Coons tuned Oldsmobile V8. In 1967 he changed over to the Repco unit. This use of Grand Prix engines in what the regulations are pleased to accept as sports cars has now spread, as might be expected, to the Ford DFV which comes next on our list.

Then came the Ford. For the second time in motoring history Ford went the whole hog for a V8. Designed by Keith Duckworth, and sponsored and provided for by Ford, the new Grand Prix engine was to sweep all before it. It was a 90° 3 litre unit with twin overhead camshafts to each bank, and developed 410hp at 9000rpm.

Here at the "launch" are the men behind it. On the left Walter Hayes, then Head of Public Affairs who backed it to the hilt as being the best affair he had heard of in a long time. Facing the camera is Sir Patrick Hennessy, boss of Ford in Britain at that time and on whose desk reposed the unwritten but traditional notice "the buck stops here". Beside him, Colin Chapman, into whose Lotus cars the engine was first to go and beside him, Graham Hill, already the doyen of Grand Prix drivers whose wisdom was more than a match for his wit – and that is saying something indeed.

The two men most concerned in the engine's construction and use were Keith Duckworth, its designer, on the right, and Colin Chapman on the left. And a shot, taken at Cosworth's factory, which could do with wider recognition. Here, flanked by two engines is Duckworth, and the men who made it all possible – not forgetting that that generic term embraces a number of ladies as well.

It would be wrong...

It would be wrong to say that victory the first time out was a foregone conclusion; but it was not all that unexpected when the driver was Jim Clark. The event, of course, was the Dutch Grand Prix of 1967, when the Scotsman beat Jack Brabham and Denny Hulme in Repco-Brabhams.

And because it helps to make the point of how small such a powerful car can be when fitted with a V8 engine – here is another shot of the same great occasion, Clark leading Hulme.

It would take a book by itself to cover the uses of the Ford V8 racing engine; but for the record, and as a representative of all the others, comes this picture of Jackie Stewart driving a Matra Ford in the 1969 Dutch Grand Prix.

If the British branch of the Ford organisation put its weight behind the Grand Prix engine, that is nothing compared with the efforts that Detroit made to win Le Mans. Having failed to "join 'em" by buying Ferrari, they set out to do the only alternative and that was to "beat 'em" – something which turned out to be easier said than done. But it was done; and in the doing came the G.T. 40 – again with a V8, but this time an American confection, though the car was planned and built very largely in Great Britain, at Slough, and under the command of that greatest of Le Mans tyros John Wyer. This is a road-going G.T. 40 of 1966.

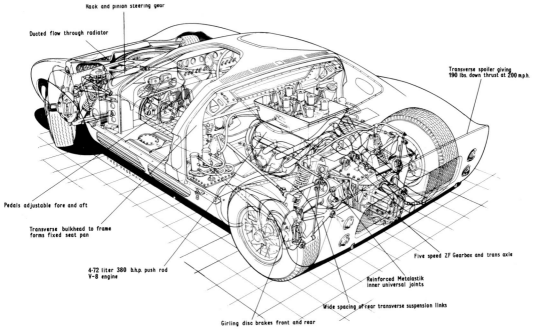

Rack and pinion steering gear

Ducted flow through radiator

Transverse spoiler giving 190 lbs. down thrust at 200 m.p.h.

Pedals adjustable fore and aft

Transverse bulkhead to frame forms fixed seat pan

Five speed ZF Gearbox and trans axle

4·72 liter 380 b.h.p. push rod V-8 engine

Reinforced Metalastik inner universal joints

Wide spacing of rear transverse suspension links

Girling disc brakes front and rear

And here it is, naked as John Donne's mistress on going to bed, and just about as well enumerated.

The engine compartment of one of the later (1967) Gulf Mirage cars which also used the American Ford V8 engine, and were, in fact, lightweight G.T. 40s sponsored by the Gulf Oil Corporation.

And of the same school but some years earlier the 1964 Lola Chevrolet. As with the Grand Prix cars, the compact nature and light weight of the V8 engine, in terms of the power produced, make it an ideal engine for exercises of this nature.

One of the sad names of history – though very far from being without success on the right day. Here is the BRM V8 on the test bed. Never, of course, as widely used as the Ford, it nevertheless found a good many customers as the ensuing pictures show.

Apart from going into BRM's own Grand Prix car it was used in the Gilby driven by Keith Greene – and provided a very neat installation. However it was never very successful, its best place being 3rd in the 1963 Rome G.P., Ian Raby driving.

And here is BRM in sports car guise, but using a
Chevrolet engine for the 1972 Can-Am series.
Evidently more than able to blow its own trumpet!

'alking of sports cars makes one realise that in many
respects they have become as complicated as the out
nd out racing cars, and certainly the Can-Am series of
aces in America and Canada have done much to foster
their development. This is a 1972 McLaren
Chevrolet – V8 of course.

A rather more unusual McLaren, is this 1969 car
powered by a Toyota V8; but not much seen outside its
native Japan. Toyota fielded a number of Can-Am type
cars powered by three and five litre V8 engines of their
own design.

Last but by no manner of means least the Chaparral –
no one has contributed more to this sphere of racing
than Jim Hall – a devotee of the V8 engine, and
inventor of countless forward thinking ideas, most of
which have been banned by the organisers before
getting accepted. Here is a Chaparral 2F at Brands
Hatch in the 1967 BOAC 500.

One of the most colourful characters to appear in British racing in the 1960s was Chris Summers. Equally at home on the sprint courses or the race track he won many events in his Cooper Chevrolet pictured here at a Sunbac club meeting at Silverstone on 1 September 1962. At that time the car was fitted with a 4.7 litre Chevrolet engine; later a 5.3 litre version was slotted in. Autosport in February 1963 wrote "many outright circuit lap records were either beaten or severely threatened by Chris Summers' wonderful hairy 4.7 litre Cooper Chevrolet. The car had a staggering ability to out-accelerate anything".

One of the prettiest and most professionally built sports car specials to be produced for hill climbing and sprinting in the early 1960s was the Farrallac, brain-child of Don Farrall. It was fitted with a 5.4 litre Cadillac engine and is seen here on the new loop (it was new then) of Prescott hill climb at a Bugatti Owners' Club meeting on 9 September 1962.

For the 1963 hill climb season in Great Britain Peter Westbury built a new car known as the "Felday". The engine was similar to the one used in his successful 1962 Cooper, namely a 2548 cc Daimler V8 running on an 8.2 to 1 compression ratio and supercharged at 8 lbs per square inch. Over 220 bhp was claimed for it. A feature of the car were the splendid megaphone exhausts pointing up into the air rather like an earlier version of the BRM. The car is seen here driven by Peter Westbury making a fastest time of the day at the British Automobile Racing Club's South Western centre, Brunton Hill Climb in June 1963.

The supercharged V8 engined "Felday" in action at a Bugatti Owners' Club hill climb at Prescott on 7 June 1964. The driver is Peter Cottrell from Pontypridd and he is seen negotiating Ettore's Bend on the extension of the hill. Due to the damp condition in the paddock the wheels and tyres are covered in mud and so the car is not looking as immaculately turned out as usual.

Jim Tiller from Brighton was a very colourful character and forceful driver in his 1950 J2 Allard, and he made many competition appearances in the 1960s and 1970s with it. This photograph was taken at a British Automobile Racing Club South Western centre hill climb at Brunton in Wiltshire on 16 June 1963. At this time his car had an engine capacity of 3917 cc and he was beaten into second place in his class by Peter Farquarson with his much larger J2X Allard and 5420 cc. Jim Tiller's car was later fitted with a 6.4 litre Cadillac engine which in 1975 had the distinction of vanquishing no less than five Ferrari Daytonas at the famous Brighton Speed Trials. For some years Jim Tiller used to tow the Allard behind his ordinary road car on a fixed self-towing bar. When the police took exception to this he fitted a very life-like dummy figure into the cockpit, fixed the hands to the steering wheel and continued to fool the law for quite some time.

Not the least of the attractions of the V8, anyway as far as the manufacturers were concerned, were those of publicity – for once the idea had caught on, and the V8 had built up its own snob connotations, it was worth crowing about.

On the following pages, as a kind of postscript, are some examples taken over a number of years. Most interestingly the first two, which are without words, picture early De Dion Bouton models. Nothing was said about the V8 although they were more or less the pioneers in Europe. The cars were identical, from the outside, with the larger six cylinder models, so that even here one can only say truthfully that they may be V8s.

Opposite them the King and the Lincoln leave no doubt, and in both cases the accent is on quality. The Apperson which follows, is now an almost forgotten make; and most people have forgotten that Talbot-Darracq made a V8. The Talbot-Darracq name is in itself interesting, for a little later the cars were called Talbots in France and Darracqs in England, so as not to confuse them with our own Talbots.

Lastly the Ford V8 which brought this kind of engine to the man in the street; and on the final page a Standard advertisement – a car from Great Britain clearly influenced by the success of the Ford – its own possible success short-lived because of the clouds of war.

EIGHT CYLINDER

King

Sole Concessionnaires:
SALMONS & SONS

Fitted with a Four-Seater Coupé body by Salmons & Sons, the King "8" Car, illustrated below, takes rank among the world's most magnificent cars. Chassis and Coachwork are worthy of each other. This model, together with a ¾ Coupé and Interior Drive Saloon Landaulette, will be on

STAND 176 WHITE CITY.

Be sure you see our Exhibits.

SALMONS & SONS
(Originators of the All-Weather Body),
6-9, Upper St. Martin's Lane, W.C.2.
WORKS : NEWPORT PAGNELL.

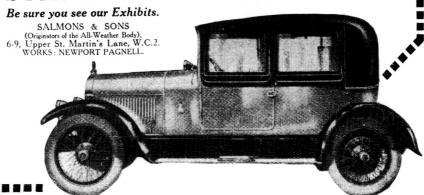

CHASSIS

The Lincoln Chassis is a masterpiece in design and construction. Outstanding features are the eight-cylinder V-type engine with cylinder block set at an included angle of 60 degrees. This arrangement causes explosions to occur at irregular intervals, which in connection with the sturdy five-bearing crank shaft, serves to reduce motor vibration to the minimum. Other features are thermostatic control of radiator shutters, improved carburation and torque tube drive, with front and rear springs shackled at both ends to relieve them of any function except that of absorbing road shock. The wheel base of the chassis is 136 inches

Apperson Eight

"The Eight with Eighty less parts"

A car of exquisite refinement

In the Apperson "Eight" is offered a car of a degree of excellence rarely met with.

You rest as you ride in it. The long wheelbase, the perfect spring suspension, and the properly tufted upholstery give a luxury of motion realised only in the Apperson.

The action of the engine may be described as "ve vety"—and achieved with the elimination of no less than eighty parts.

The car smoothly accelerates from four to forty miles in forty yards, and drops to a standstill in four seconds in the same distance.

It is a car of high performance—more than equal to all general conditions of travel.

Melchior, Armstrong & Dessau
(LONDON) LTD.

14B, Gt. Marlborough St.,
London, W.1.

Telegrams: "Willdegre, London."
Telephone: Not yet obtainable.

THE NEW EIGHT-CYLINDER

TALBOT-DARRACQ

will be exhibited at

STAND No. 90
OLYMPIA Nov. 7th to 15th.

Do not miss the opportunity of making a thorough examination of this latest masterpiece in eight-cylinder design and construction.

The Darracq Motor Engineering Co., Ltd., **Townmead Road, Fulham, London, S.W. 6.**
West End Showrooms: 150, New Bond Street, W. 1.

THE FORD V-8 FOR 1937 IS OFFERED WI[TH]

Two Great V-8 Engine[s]

85 HORSEPOWER   **60 HORSEPOWE[R]**

REACHING NEW "HIGHS" IN ECONOMY

The advantages of bringing the V-type 8-cylinder engine to the lowest price field have been proved in the hands of nearly four million Ford V-8 owners. To extend these advantages still further and to provide even higher standards of economical operation, the Ford V-8 engine this year is built in two sizes.

The 85-horsepower Ford V-8 has been designed to give maximum performance. It is the engine which has put Ford performance in a class by itself. Yet from year to year, improved carburetion with added engine and chassis refinements have contributed toward better and better gasoline economy—without sacrificing the flashing speed and acceleration that are associated with the Ford V-8.

The new 60-horsepower V-8 engine was designed especially to give maximum economy—with smooth, power[ful] performance that covers the full range of many driv[ing] needs. It is smaller and lighter, making two advanta[ges] possible: (1) higher gasoline mileage without sacrific[ing] roominess or comfort—many owners report twenty-[five] to twenty-seven miles to the gallon. (2) The lowest price [for] a Ford car in years.

Whether you select the "85" or the "60", you get all [the] benefits of a quality V-8 engine—compactness, smoothne[ss,] reliability. And you get this quality engine at low cost in [the] Ford alone. It is the heart of "The Quality Car in the Lo[w] Price Field"—providing the thrifty way to travel first cla[ss.]

HERE IS THE
FLYING STANDARD "V-EIGHT"
SUPERB NEW MODEL WITH MAGNIFICENT PERFORMANCE

Here is the Flying Standard "V-Eight," introduced at Olympia, the latest production of The Standard Motor Co. Ltd. All the luxury and beauty of Flying Standard bodywork—plus the amazing road performance provided by an entirely new V-type 8-cylinder engine developing 75 h.p. at 4,000 r.p.m.   82 m.p.h. on top gear! 60 m.p.h. on 3rd gear! Whilst the car will accelerate from 0-50 m.p.h. through the gears in 12 seconds!   And this with faultless roadholding—exceptionally rigid chassis construction, with the new feature, "torsion bars," at front and rear, provide steadiness and stability on all types of road surfaces. With beautiful looks and every luxurious appointment, the Flying Standard "V-Eight" may well prove to be the most outstanding car produced in Great Britain of recent years.

SALOON DE LUXE - £349 *ex works.*

DROP - HEAD COUPÉ £359 *ex works.*

(For particulars see separate leaflet).

SANTO RADIO *can be fitted to either model for a charge of* **£13** *extra.*

The latest development of the famous Cosworth/Ford V8 powers this 1978 Lotus in which Mario Andretti won the world championship. It is an interesting sidelight that the pundits have been saying for the past five years or so, that the V8 is finished and must give way to the twelve; but so far it has not been proved in any way inferior.

Index